GET OUT
of that
PIT

A 40-DAY DEVOTIONAL
JOURNAL

BETH MOORE

W PUBLISHING GROUP

An Imprint of Thomas Nelson

Get Out of That Pit: A 40-Day Devotional Journal

Published in Nashville, Tennessee, by W Publishing, an imprint of Thomas Nelson.

Published in association with Yates & Yates, www.yates2.com.

Thomas Nelson titles may be purchased in bulk for educational, business, fundraising, or sales promotional use. For information, please e-mail SpecialMarkets@ThomasNelson.com.

ISBN 978-1-4003-3610-4

Library of Congress Cataloging-in-Publication Data

Moore, Beth, 1957–
Get out of that pit: a 40-day devotional journal / Beth Moore.
p. cm.
Includes bibliographical references.
ISBN 978-0-8499-9155-4 (hardcover)
1. Christian life. 2. Devotional literature. I. Title.
BV4501.3.M6543 2007
242'.2—dc22
2007027907

Printed in the United States of America

23 24 25 26 27 LBC 5 4 3 2 1

To Kendall, Courtney, Claire, and Kelly—

When God first awakened a very special place in my heart
for you, darling Kendall, I had no idea how much I'd
come to love all three of your little sisters too. All four of
you are bright sunshine on a Sunday morning at church
and heaping helpings of strawberry shortcake at lunch.
Never let life talk you into a pit. God has too wonderful
a plan for each of you to waste a moment of it in defeat.
Thank you for bringing so many smiles into my life.

I'm crazy about you!

Miss Beth

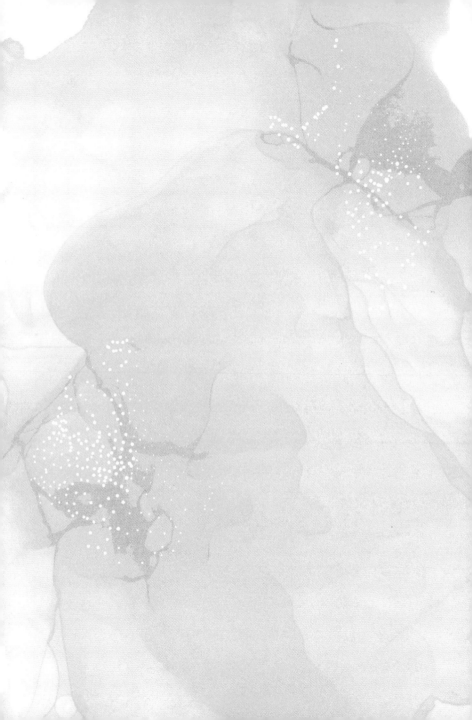

CONTENTS

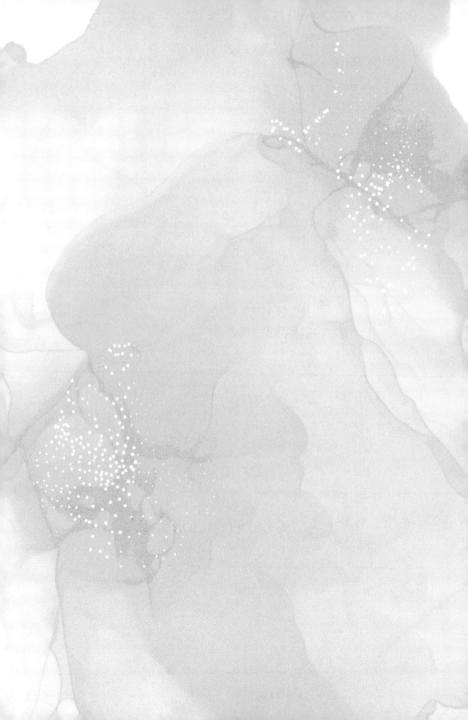

ACKNOWLEDGMENTS

In addition to all those who contributed to the original format of *Get Out of That Pit*, I owe and will joyfully pay a deep debt of gratitude to my beloved firstborn, Amanda Jones. This message comes to you in this form because of her hard work. She reformatted the book into forty autonomous journal entries complete with Scripture readings and questions as only someone could do who shares the same passion. I trust Amanda so thoroughly that hers are the first eyes that see anything I've written. A rare concoction of smart and sweet, Amanda's encouragements, gentle edits, and cultural insights continually prove invaluable to me. I am blessed beyond measure that she was the first little creature to ever call me *Mom*.

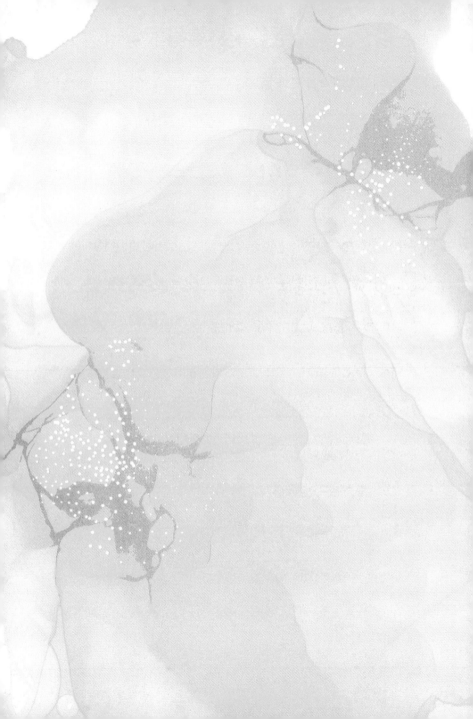

INTRODUCTION

Life can be excruciating. Crushing, in fact. The sheer magnitude of our worries can press down on our heads until we unknowingly descend into a pit of despair one inch at a time. Something so horrible can happen that we conclude we'll never be okay again. We can blow it so badly we think God would just as soon we stayed under the dirt and out of His sight. But, if we're willing to let truth speak louder than our feelings, and long enough that our feelings finally agree, we can be far more than okay. We can be delivered to a place where the air is crisp, the Enemy is whipped, and the view is magnificent.

And not just for a day or two. We're talking about living the rest of our lives out of the pit and in the fresh air and bright light of God's will.

Perhaps you've been in a hole so long you can't imagine escaping and never returning. Truth be told, you'd just settle for a few days of relief. You see, if you're like me, somewhere along the way, pit-dwelling became habitual. Homey. But former pit-dwellers like me have to form a new habit that leads to a new place to call home.

That's exactly where the book you hold in your hands comes

into play. A life of consistent victory happens one day at a time. I'd love to have the privilege of walking you through forty of them. Biblically speaking, forty days is time enough to have endured some periods of testing and proven yourself victorious. And by the time they're complete, I pray you'll have a new habit you intend never to give up.

Each section of this devotional corresponds to a chapter in the original book. And each devotional day in this book contains four parts: a devotional reading, a reflection question, a personal application question, and a page for prayer journaling. The "Reflection Question" page will highlight the main point of the day while the "Personal Application" page will relate the material to your own life and circumstances. Since writing out your answers can reinforce what God is showing you, space is provided for you to put on paper the answer to each question.

The journal page, "Reaching Up," is a place for you to pen your prayers to God. Each day when you arrive at this crucial conclusion, picture this metaphor: every time you cry out to God and you agree to cooperate with His great work of deliverance, you are reaching up your hand to grab hold of His strong arm. That, beloved, is the way out of the pit. If we could see with spiritual eyes, we'd probably see years of accumulated dirt underneath our fingernails from trying to claw our way out of the pit. Give it up. God is already reaching His hand into that hole. Learn how to reach up and grab on for dear life.

If you're willing to hear, God has much to say to you through the pages of this book. Remember, though, the essence of relationship is two-way communication. He'll speak to you if you'll let Him, but He'll also want you to speak to Him. The most glorious outcome of your journey from the pit will be the new relationship you've formed with the Deliverer. The deliverance is the means to a far greater end.

You and I won't find a perfect place to live on this planet, but never let anybody tell you life can't be lived *well.* We can live the rest of our days out of a pit. Our problems won't disappear. Nor will our temptations vanish. But Psalm 27:5–6 can be just as true of us as it was of the psalmist. In the day of trouble, God can set us high upon a rock where our heads are exalted above the enemies who surround us, and, right there amid our circumstances, we can overcome every assault with shouts of joy, making music to the Lord.

Life can be different, beloved, but not if we keep putting change off until tomorrow. A day has to come when we're ready to say, "Today." How about this one?

I'll meet you on Day One . . .

Love, Beth

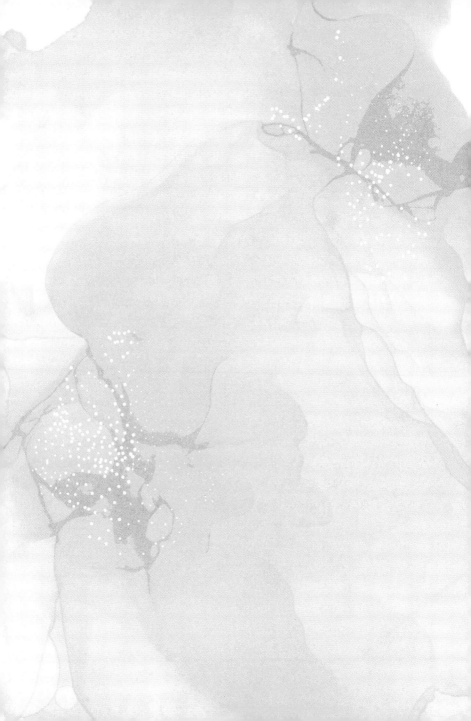

DAY 1

Come, Follow Me

From the ends of the earth I call to you,
I call as my heart grows faint;
lead me to the rock that is higher than I.
—PSALM 61:2

You don't have to stay in the pit. Even if you deserve it. Even if you've known nothing else. Just call it a day. Maybe you're wondering why you can't get satisfied there. After all, didn't Paul say we should learn to be content in any circumstance?

A pit is one place you're not supposed to be content. Quit trying to make the best of it. It's time to get out. When Christ said, "Come, follow me," inherent in His invitation to come was the equivalent invitation to leave. The laws of physics tell you that if you try to get one place without leaving another, you're in for a pretty severe stretch. And you can only do the splits so long.

Reflection Question

When Christ said, "Come, follow me," there was
something inherent in His invitation. What was it?

....

_____

_____

_____

_____

_____

_____

_____

_____

_____

_____

_____

_____

_____

_____

_____

_____

_____

_____

"Come, follow me," Jesus said, "and I will send you out to fish for people."

—MARK 1:17

Personal Application

What hope do the words of Psalm 40 offer you
personally in terms of the pit you may be in?

• •

_____

_____

_____

_____

_____

_____

_____

_____

_____

_____

_____

_____

_____

_____

_____

_____

_____

_____

_____

But thanks be to God, who always leads us as captives
in Christ's triumphal procession and uses us to spread
the aroma of the knowledge of him everywhere.
—2 CORINTHIANS 2:14

Reaching Up

••••••••••••••••••••••••••••••••••

Bondage Blended In

Here a great number of disabled people used to lie—the blind, the lame, the paralyzed. One who was there had been an invalid for thirty-eight years. When Jesus saw him lying there and learned that he had been in this condition for a long time, he asked him, "Do you want to get well?"

—JOHN 5:3-6

No matter where we go, a pit can always fit. On any path we can spin our wheels and throw mud until we dig a ditch right into the middle of an otherwise decent job or relationship. Soon our hearts sink with the dismal realization that we're no better off in our new situation. The scenery around us may have changed, but we're still living in that same old pit. We start scrambling to figure out how we're going to dump an unpleasant person or position when the real solution may be to dump that pit we dragged in. The problem is the pit can be so close we can't see it.

Reflection Question

For some people, a pit can be so close they
can't see it. Why is this true?

• •

_____

_____

_____

_____

_____

_____

_____

_____

_____

_____

_____

_____

_____

_____

_____

_____

_____

_____

It is for freedom that Christ has set us free.

—GALATIANS 5:1

Personal Application

Have you ever been—or are you now—a "mobile pit-dweller"? If so, what was/is the nature of your mobile pit, and where did/do you take it?

·······································

_____

_____

_____

_____

_____

_____

_____

_____

_____

_____

_____

_____

_____

_____

_____

_____

_____

_____

Stand firm, then, and do not let yourselves be
burdened again by a yoke of slavery.
—GALATIANS 5:1

Reaching Up

....

_____

_____

_____

_____

_____

_____

_____

_____

_____

_____

_____

_____

_____

_____

_____

_____

_____

_____

_____

_____

_____

_____

_____

_____

_____

A New Home

"No one sews a patch of unshrunk cloth on an old garment, for the patch will pull away from the garment, making the tear worse. Neither do people pour new wine into old wineskins. If they do, the skins will burst, the wine will run out and the wineskins will be ruined. No, they pour new wine into new wineskins, and both are preserved."

—MATTHEW 9:16–17

We can grow so accustomed to the surroundings of our pit that we wouldn't think of moving on without it. Imagine you've been living in an old RV so small you can't stand up straight. There's clutter everywhere. The lavatory smells, but you've gotten used to it.

Now, imagine that you've been offered a brand-new home on a solid foundation with big closets and wide-open spaces. You rev up the motor of the old RV and plow it right into the new living room. A new place to call home! You settle back in your RV seat, take a deep breath, and poise yourself to feel something fresh.

But that breath tasted a lot like that old lavatory.

Reflection Question

The amusing illustration of a person driving an RV into the living room of her new home makes an important point. What is it?

● ●

_____

_____

_____

_____

_____

_____

_____

_____

_____

_____

_____

_____

_____

_____

_____

_____

_____

_____

Therefore, if anyone is in Christ, the new creation has
come: The old has gone, the new is here!
—2 CORINTHIANS 5:17

Personal Application

Some of us recognize our pits not by the degree of our badness but by the degree of our boredom. Reflect on the degree of boredom in your own life and whether or not it's an indication that you may be in a pit.

••••••••••••••••••••••••••••••••••

_____

_____

_____

_____

_____

_____

_____

_____

_____

_____

_____

_____

_____

_____

Yet I hold this against you: You have forsaken the love
you had at first. Consider how far you have fallen!
Repent and do the things you did at first.
—REVELATION 2:4–5

Reaching Up

· ·

You're in a Pit When . . .

So they took Jeremiah and put him into the cistern of Malkijah,
the king's son, which was in the courtyard of the guard. They
lowered Jeremiah by ropes into the cistern; it had no water in
it, only mud, and Jeremiah sank down into the mud.

—JEREMIAH 38:6

You're in a pit when . . .

- You feel stuck. You feel you can only have a kicking and screaming fit or submit.
- You can't stand up. You feel ineffective and utterly powerless against the Enemy's attack.
- You've lost vision. Unlike that rank old RV, pits have no windows. The darkness impairs your sight.

Without windows, you're convinced you have nowhere else to go. You could look up, but you're too busy looking at your sinking feet. You become what the Bible calls stiff-necked. The confinement exhausts you with the endless echo of self-absorption. You can't see out, so you turn your sights in. Nearsightedness breeds hopelessness. You feel too buried in your present state to feel passionate about a promised future.

Reflection Question

Often we don't recognize a pit when we're in
one. What three signs characterize a pit? In other
words, you know you're in a pit when . . .

· ·

_____

_____

_____

_____

_____

_____

_____

_____

_____

_____

_____

_____

_____

_____

I sink in the miry depths,
where there is no foothold.
I have come into the deep waters;
the floods engulf me.
—PSALM 69:2

Personal Application

"The close confinement of a pit exhausts us with the endless echo of self-absorption." Do you resonate with this statement? If so, why?

••••••••••••••••••••••••••••••••••••

_____

_____

_____

_____

_____

_____

_____

_____

_____

_____

_____

_____

_____

_____

_____

_____

_____

Even though we speak like this, dear friends, we are convinced of better things in your case—the things that have to do with salvation.

—HEBREWS 6:9

Reaching Up

....

_____

_____

_____

_____

_____

_____

_____

_____

_____

_____

_____

_____

_____

_____

_____

_____

_____

_____

_____

_____

_____

_____

DAY 5

You Can Get Thrown In

They saw him in the distance, and before he had reached them, they plotted to kill him. They said to one another, "Here comes that dreamer! Come on, let's kill him and throw him into one of the pits. We can say that a vicious animal ate him. Then we'll see what becomes of his dreams!"
—GENESIS 37:18–20 HCSB

You can get thrown into a pit. That's right, without doing one thing to deserve it and without wallowing your way into it. I'm not talking about a pit of sin here. This one's a pit of innocence—the kind a lot of believers don't realize exists. You can get thrown right into the miry deep before you know what hit you. Or worse yet, *who* hit you. In fact, those were the circumstances surrounding the first pit ever mentioned in Scripture. In a fit of jealous rage set up by their father's partiality, the older sons of Jacob threw their seventeen-year-old little brother, Joseph, into a cistern with the intention of leaving him for dead.

Let that sink in a second.

Reflection Question

We can be thrown into "pits of innocence." Give some
examples of ways innocent people are thrown into pits.

••••••••••••••••••••••••••••••••••••

_____

_____

_____

_____

_____

_____

_____

_____

_____

_____

_____

_____

_____

_____

_____

_____

_____

When Joseph came to his brothers, they stripped off his robe,
the robe of many colors that he had on. Then they took him
and threw him into the pit. The pit was empty; there was
no water in it. Then they sat down to eat a meal.

—GENESIS 37:23–25 HCSB

Personal Application

If someone has thrown you into a pit of innocence, where are you now in terms of getting out and finding that "firm place to stand" that the psalmist talked about? Stuck in the mud and mire? Working your way out? Standing on a rock? Explain your answer.

••••••••••••••••••••••••••••••••••

_____

_____

_____

_____

_____

_____

_____

_____

_____

_____

_____

Do not take revenge, my friends, but leave room for God's wrath, for it is written: "It is mine to avenge; I will repay," says the Lord. On the contrary:
"If your enemy is hungry, feed him;
if he is thirsty, give him something to drink.
In doing this, you will heap burning coals on his head."

Do not be overcome by evil, but overcome evil with good.
—ROMANS 12:19–21

Reaching Up

· ·

_____

_____

_____

_____

_____

_____

_____

_____

_____

_____

_____

_____

_____

_____

_____

_____

_____

_____

_____

_____

_____

_____

Complications

Then Jacob tore his clothes, put on sackcloth and mourned for his son many days. All his sons and daughters came to comfort him, but he refused to be comforted. "No," he said, "I will continue to mourn until I join my son in the grave." So his father wept for him.

—GENESIS 37:34-35

Getting thrown into a pit by another person can be the most complicated scenario to deal with. Having someone to blame can eat us alive! Oftentimes, we know in our heart that it wasn't his or her intention. Take, for instance, a family member with mental illness, or a parent who neglects her healthy children because she can't help focusing on one handicapped child. What if we've been thrown in by the sin of another person—perhaps a family member? Joseph's brothers sat down to eat a meal while he surely screamed from the pit nearby. What about when the person remains close by, lives on as if nothing has ever happened, sees our distress and anguish, but will not hear us?

Reflection Question

A pit we are thrown into can be the most complicated
to deal with, emotionally and spiritually. Why?

••••••••••••••••••••••••••••••••••

_____

_____

_____

_____

_____

_____

_____

_____

_____

_____

_____

_____

_____

_____

_____

_____

Commit your way to the LORD;
trust in him and he will do this:
He will make your righteous reward shine like the dawn,
your vindication like the noonday sun.

—PSALM 37:5-6

Personal Application

Have you ever felt "comfortable" living in a pit? If so, why was this true for you at the time?

•••••••••••••••••••••••••••••••••••••

_____

_____

_____

_____

_____

_____

_____

_____

_____

_____

_____

_____

_____

_____

_____

_____

_____

Be still before the Lord
and wait patiently for him;
do not fret when people succeed in their ways,
when they carry out their wicked schemes.
—PSALM 37:7

Reaching Up

....

_____

_____

_____

_____

_____

_____

_____

_____

_____

_____

_____

_____

_____

_____

_____

_____

_____

_____

_____

_____

_____

From a Pit of Innocence to a Pit of Sin

Bear with each other and forgive one another if any of you has a grievance against someone. Forgive as the Lord forgave you.
—COLOSSIANS 3:13

I hate to bring up this word, but I just don't have a choice: forgive. It's tough to do, but we've got to forgive, even—no, especially— those who don't care to be forgiven. Forgive them not only for their destructiveness, but also for their *ignorance*. They don't have a clue how much it affected your decisions and relationships. I'm not sure they would get it even if you told them in detail upon detail.

I started out in a pit of innocence, but eventually my bitterness rearranged the furniture until it was nothing more than a pit of sin. I thought forgiving my pit-throwers would make what they did all right. But it didn't. Forgiveness made *me* all right.

Reflection Question

Sometimes we start out in a pit of innocence, but later
find ourselves in a pit of sin. What is the potential
sin of a person who has been thrown in a pit?

. . . .

_____

_____

_____

_____

_____

_____

_____

_____

_____

_____

_____

_____

_____

_____

_____

*For if you forgive other people when they sin against you, your
heavenly Father will also forgive you. But if you do not forgive
others their sins, your Father will not forgive your sins.*

—MATTHEW 6:14–15

Personal Application

Has the "willingness" and "power" of forgiveness
ever been something you have experienced? If so,
describe the circumstances and the outcome.

••••••••••••••••••••••••••••••••••••

_____

_____

_____

_____

_____

_____

_____

_____

_____

_____

_____

_____

_____

_____

_____

*Then Peter came to Jesus and asked, "Lord, how many times shall I
forgive my brother or sister who sins against me? Up to seven times?"
Jesus answered, "I tell you, not seven times, but seventy-seven times."*
—MATTHEW 18:21-22

Reaching Up

....

_____
_____
_____
_____
_____
_____
_____
_____
_____
_____
_____
_____
_____
_____
_____
_____
_____
_____
_____
_____
_____
_____
_____
_____
_____

The Responsible Party

But Joseph said to them, "Don't be afraid. Am I in the place
of God? You intended to harm me, but God intended it for
good to accomplish what is now being done, the saving of many
lives. So then, don't be afraid. I will provide for you and your
children." And he reassured them and spoke kindly to them.

—GENESIS 50:19–21

Joseph eventually decided not only to look up but also to point up. His decision to view God as entirely sovereign and ultimately responsible was the life of him, not the death of him. Why? Because he knew God could only be good and do right. Joseph's words to his brothers have been medicine to many sick souls who were willing to swallow them whole: "You intended to harm me, but God intended it for good to accomplish what is now being done, the saving of many lives" (Genesis 50:20). God saw the good it could ultimately accomplish, the lives that could be helped and even saved. Had the incident not possessed glorious purpose, God would have disarmed it.

Reflection Question

Holding God ultimately responsible in the healthy way
His Word suggests will be our ticket out of a pit. What
is this healthy way? Read Genesis 50:20 to discover how
Joseph found a healthy way to hold God responsible.

• •

_____

_____

_____

_____

_____

_____

_____

_____

_____

_____

_____

_____

_____

*In all this you greatly rejoice, though now for a little while you
may have had to suffer grief in all kinds of trials. These have come
so that the proven genuineness of your faith—of greater worth
than gold, which perishes even though refined by fire—may result
in praise, glory and honor when Jesus Christ is revealed.*

—1 PETER 1:6-7

Personal Application

"Your wealth of experience makes you rich. Spend it on people."
How might God use your suffering to help or heal others?

• •

_____

_____

_____

_____

_____

_____

_____

_____

_____

_____

_____

_____

_____

_____

_____

_____

_____

_____

And we know that in all things God works for the good of those
who love him, who have been called according to his purpose.

—ROMANS 8:28

Reaching Up

....

_____

_____

_____

_____

_____

_____

_____

_____

_____

_____

_____

_____

_____

_____

_____

_____

_____

_____

_____

_____

_____

_____

DAY 9

You Can Slip In

For troubles without number surround me;
my sins have overtaken me, and I cannot see.
They are more than the hairs of my head,
and my heart fails within me.
Be pleased to save me, LORD;
come quickly, LORD, to help me.
—PSALM 40:12–13

You can slip into a pit. Unlike the pit we get thrown into, we put ourselves into this one. But we didn't mean to. We just weren't watching where we were going. We got a little distracted, taken in by the new sights. The path didn't seem bad; it just seemed new. Exhilarating. We thought we were still okay, but the next thing we knew we were in a hole, our feet ankle-deep in mud.

You got into this pit yourself, but it wasn't planned. Or wanted. Falling into a pit may have never entered your mind. You certainly didn't mean for things to turn out the way they did. You didn't see it coming, but now you're in a hole.

Reflection Question

What are several ways a person might slip into a pit?

••••••••••••••••••••••••••••••••••

_____

_____

_____

_____

_____

_____

_____

_____

_____

_____

_____

_____

_____

_____

_____

My guilt has overwhelmed me
like a burden too heavy to bear.
My wounds fester and are loathsome
because of my sinful folly.
I am bowed down and brought very low;
all day long I go about mourning.
—PSALM 38:4-6

Personal Application

Read Psalm 38:4–6, 9, 12, and 14–17. Think of a time
when you slid into a pit, and underline the words in
those verses that describe how you felt (or feel now)
about the situation in which you found (or find) yourself.
Then expand on those words and feelings here.

· ·

_____

_____

_____

_____

_____

_____

_____

_____

I have become like one who does not hear,
whose mouth can offer no reply.
Lord, I wait for you;
you will answer, Lord my God.
For I said, "Do not let them gloat
or exalt themselves over me when my feet slip."
For I am about to fall,
and my pain is ever with me.
—PSALM 38:14–17

Reaching Up

....

_____

_____

_____

_____

_____

_____

_____

_____

_____

_____

_____

_____

_____

_____

_____

_____

_____

_____

_____

_____

_____

_____

_____

Satan's Step-by-Step Plan

Finally, be strong in the Lord and in his mighty power. Put on the full armor of God, so that you can take your stand against the devil's schemes. For our struggle is not against flesh and blood, but against the rulers, against the authorities, against the powers of this dark world and against the spiritual forces of evil in the heavenly realms.
—EPHESIANS 6:10–12

Distraction ⇨ Addiction ⇨ Destruction

Satan aims to destroy, but that's rarely his starting point. His usual opening is *distraction*. But he won't allow a new focus to remain a distraction. The next step is *addiction*. It is a highly effective way to turn something we *have* (a sin-induced problem) into some place we *live* (a sin-induced pit). Defeat becomes a lifestyle. Satan is smug about his progress at this point but remember, addiction is not his goal. *Destruction* is. He wants to destroy our lives, callings, sense of godly significance, meaningful relationships, and intimacy with God.

Listen carefully: if you belong to Christ, Satan cannot destroy you. He can only convince you that you're destroyed. No, beloved, you're not.

Reflection Question

What is Satan's three-step progressive
plan to get us to slip into a pit?

• •

_____

_____

_____

_____

_____

_____

_____

_____

_____

_____

_____

_____

_____

_____

_____

If I should say, "My foot has slipped,"
Your lovingkindness, O LORD, will hold me up.
When my anxious thoughts multiply within me
Your consolations delight my soul.
—PSALM 94:18–19 NASB

Personal Application

Are you now in the "distraction" phase of a
potential pit? If so, what is the Holy Spirit saying
to you? What do you need to do now?

••••••••••••••••••••••••••••••••••

_____

_____

_____

_____

_____

_____

_____

_____

_____

_____

_____

_____

_____

_____

_____

_____

_____

_____

*We are hard pressed on every side, but not crushed; perplexed, but not in
despair; persecuted, but not abandoned; struck down, but not destroyed.*
—2 CORINTHIANS 4:8-9

Reaching Up

....

_____

_____

_____

_____

_____

_____

_____

_____

_____

_____

_____

_____

_____

_____

_____

_____

_____

_____

_____

_____

_____

_____

From Distraction to Stronghold

The weapons we fight with are not the weapons of the world. On the contrary, they have divine power to demolish strongholds. We demolish arguments and every pretension that sets itself up against the knowledge of God, and we take captive every thought to make it obedient to Christ.

—2 CORINTHIANS 10:4-5

A small distraction that becomes a big distraction is a *stronghold* for the devil. Scripture defines it as any and "every pretension that sets itself up against the knowledge of God" (2 Corinthians 10:5). Anything that becomes a bigger preoccupation in your mind than the truth and knowledge of God, anything that dwarfs His truth and knowledge in your imagination, is a stronghold. If a relationship keeps me from prioritizing Christ and His Word, Satan is building a stronghold there. If watching what I eat becomes a major preoccupation rather than a means to better health, Satan is building a stronghold. If a same-sex friendship takes on a dimension of jealousy usually limited to a male-female romance, Satan is building a stronghold.

Reflection Question

Scripture has a name for a small distraction that
becomes a big distraction. What is it?

· ·

_____

_____

_____

_____

_____

_____

_____

_____

_____

_____

_____

_____

_____

_____

*They are darkened in their understanding and separated from
the life of God because of the ignorance that is in them due
to the hardening of their hearts. Having lost all sensitivity,
they have given themselves over to sensuality so as to indulge
in every kind of impurity, and they are full of greed.*
—EPHESIANS 4:18–19

Personal Application

What are some tricks Satan uses to distract
you into sliding into sin?

· ·

_____

_____

_____

_____

_____

_____

_____

_____

_____

_____

_____

_____

_____

_____

*I am jealous for you with a godly jealousy. I promised you to one husband,
to Christ, so that I might present you as a pure virgin to him. But I am
afraid that just as Eve was deceived by the serpent's cunning, your minds
may somehow be led astray from your sincere and pure devotion to Christ.*
—2 CORINTHIANS 11:2–3

Reaching Up

....

_____

_____

_____

_____

_____

_____

_____

_____

_____

_____

_____

_____

_____

_____

_____

_____

_____

_____

_____

_____

_____

_____

_____

DAY 12

A Built-In Alarm

He has delivered us from such a deadly peril, and he will deliver us
again. On him we have set our hope that he will continue to deliver us.
—2 CORINTHIANS 1:10

One day my friend heard a beeper going off inside her house. She thought it was her husband's and began looking for it. No matter where she looked, the sound was the same. Imagine her surprise when she finally realized that the beep was coming from inside of her. The battery on her pacemaker was going out and sounding an alarm. She didn't even know the pacemaker had an alarm.

If you're in Christ, you have a built-in alarm system. The Holy Spirit is in us, and if we don't quench Him He'll tell us early on when we're headed for trouble. He'll also tell us whether to be careful right where we are or to bail out altogether.

Reflection Question

What is the Christian's built-in "alarm system" against slipping into sin? How does that alarm system work in a person's life?

....

_____

_____

_____

_____

_____

_____

_____

_____

_____

_____

_____

_____

_____

_____

_____

_____

_____

_____

You, dear children, are from God and have overcome them, because the one who is in you is greater than the one who is in the world.

—1 JOHN 4:4

Personal Application

If you were in Christ at the time of Satan's first distraction, when did the Holy Spirit first sound an alarm? How did you respond?

••••••••••••••••••••••••••••••••••••

_____

_____

_____

_____

_____

_____

_____

_____

_____

_____

_____

_____

_____

_____

_____

_____

_____

_____

You provide a broad path for my feet,
so that my ankles do not give way.
—PSALM 18:36

Reaching Up

....

_____

_____

_____

_____

_____

_____

_____

_____

_____

_____

_____

_____

_____

_____

_____

_____

_____

_____

_____

_____

_____

_____

_____

DAY 13

You Can Jump In

Keep your servant also from willful sins;
may they not rule over me.
Then will I be blameless,
innocent of great transgression.
—PSALM 19:13

You can jump in—that's the third and final way you can land in a pit. Before you take the plunge into that pit, you can be well aware that what you're about to do is wrong, probably even foolish. But the escalating desire to do it exceeds the good sense not to. You had time to think, and then you did exactly what you meant to do even if the pit turned out to be deeper and the consequences higher than you hoped.

You, like me, probably do what you do because you want to. You like the trip. You don't necessarily like the cost but, like all vacations, a great trip can be worth the expense.

Reflection Question

The third way we can get into a pit is by jumping in. How does this method differ from the other two, especially in terms of the motive and mindset of the person who jumps?

• •

_____

_____

_____

_____

_____

_____

_____

_____

_____

_____

_____

_____

_____

_____

"God does all these things to a person—
twice, even three times—
to turn them back from the pit,
that the light of life may shine on them.

—JOB 33:29-30

Personal Application

Each of us will ultimately do what we want to do. Christ asks, "What do you want, Child?" How will you answer that question?

•••••••••••••••••••••••••••••••••

_____

_____

_____

_____

_____

_____

_____

_____

_____

_____

_____

_____

_____

_____

_____

_____

_____

_____

_____

*Though we are slaves, our God has not forsaken us in our bondage.
He has shown us kindness in the sight of the kings of Persia: He has
granted us new life to rebuild the house of our God and repair its ruins,
and he has given us a wall of protection in Judah and Jerusalem.*

—EZRA 9:9

Reaching Up

·······································

_____

_____

_____

_____

_____

_____

_____

_____

_____

_____

_____

_____

_____

_____

_____

_____

_____

_____

_____

_____

_____

_____

DAY 14

Dangerous Territory

Do not be deceived: God cannot be mocked. A man reaps what he
sows. Whoever sows to please their flesh, from the flesh will reap
destruction; whoever sows to please the Spirit, from the Spirit will
reap eternal life. Let us not become weary in doing good, for at
the proper time we will reap a harvest if we do not give up.
—GALATIANS 6:7–9

The problem with us pit-jumpers is that we don't want to hear God's warnings when we get close to a pit. We want what we want. So we stick our fingers in our ears before we jump. This is by far the most dangerous and supremely consequential way to get in a pit. Motive is huge to God. And so is character. Primarily His character, which we are created to emulate. And He will not be mocked. The very segment of Scripture where we're told God won't be mocked is strategically centered in the context of reaping what we sow (see Galatians 6:7–9). God looks intently not only at what we've done and how, but also *why* we did it.

Reflection Question

Why is "jumping in" the most dangerous and supremely
consequential method of getting into a pit?

••••••••••••••••••••••••••••••••••••

Wash and make yourselves clean.
Take your evil deeds out of my sight;
stop doing wrong.
Learn to do right.
—ISAIAH 1:16–17

Personal Application

The psalmist said, "I delight to do Your will, my God; / Your Law is within my heart" (Psalm 40:8 NASB). On a continuum between "not at all" to "yes, I'm there," how true is this for you today?

••••••••••••••••••••••••••••••••

_____
_____
_____
_____
_____
_____
_____
_____
_____
_____
_____
_____
_____

As obedient children, do not conform to the evil desires
you had when you lived in ignorance. But just as he
who called you is holy, so be holy in all you do.
—1 PETER 1:14–15

Reaching Up

....

DAY 15

Deformed Desire

Such a person feeds on ashes; a deluded heart misleads him;
he cannot save himself, or say,
"Is not this thing in my right hand a lie?"
—ISAIAH 44:20

When tempted, no one should say, 'God is tempting me.' For God cannot be tempted by evil, nor does he tempt anyone; but each person is tempted when they are dragged away by their own evil desire and enticed. Then, after desire has conceived, it gives birth to sin; and sin, when it is full-grown, gives birth to death" (James 1:13–15). The *New American Commentary* defines *epithumia*, the Greek word translated "evil desire," as a "deformed desire." Deformed desire is what I had. I often hated what I wanted and wished I didn't want it. Still, desire—deformed and destructive—lurched and led. I didn't realize my heart was sick. My messed-up "want to" was tremendously unhealthy and self-destructive.

Reflection Question

What is a "deformed desire"?

••••••••••••••••••••••••••••••••••••

_____

_____

_____

_____

_____

_____

_____

_____

_____

_____

_____

_____

_____

_____

_____

_____

_____

_____

_____

_____

Create in me a pure heart, O God,
and renew a steadfast spirit within me.

—PSALM 51:10

Personal Application

"We are so perfectly fitted for passion that we will find it one way or another. If we don't find it in Christ, we'll find it in things like lust, anger, rage, and greed." How have you seen this truth displayed in your own life or in the lives of those you know?

••••••••••••••••••••••••••••••••••

_____

_____

_____

_____

_____

_____

_____

_____

_____

_____

_____

I will give you a new heart and put a new spirit in you; I
will remove from you your heart of stone and give you a
heart of flesh. And I will put my Spirit in you and move you
to follow my decrees and be careful to keep my laws.

—EZEKIEL 36:26–27

Reaching Up

....

_____

_____

_____

_____

_____

_____

_____

_____

_____

_____

_____

_____

_____

_____

_____

_____

_____

_____

_____

_____

_____

A Saving "No"

Dear friends, I urge you, as foreigners and exiles, to abstain
from sinful desires, which wage war against your soul.
—1 PETER 2:11

God's "no" is a quick shove away from a pit. The sooner, the better. I didn't begin to live in victory just because all opportunity to jump finally disappeared. God worked with me and built trust in me until finally I'd go where He pointed. That's been our *modus operandi* for a while, but He's wise never to let me forget the excruciating pain of where I've been . . . lest I be tempted to go back.

Until we're nine-tenths in the grave, none of us is past the danger of a pit. Quick carnal impulses leap into all of our heads at times, but once we've let God win our hearts, a high tide of holy desire can wash them away.

Reflection Question

What one word does God use as His quickest
way to shove us away from the pit?

••••••••••••••••••••••••••••••••••••

_____

_____

_____

_____

_____

_____

_____

_____

_____

_____

_____

_____

_____

"Listen to me, you who pursue righteousness
and who seek the LORD:
Look to the rock from which you were cut
and to the quarry from which you were hewn.
—ISAIAH 51:1

Personal Application

Why is God wise to never let you forget the
excruciating pain of where you've been?

• •

_____

_____

_____

_____

_____

_____

_____

_____

_____

_____

_____

_____

_____

_____

_____

_____

_____

_____

I desire to do your will, my God;
your law is within my heart.
—PSALM 40:8

Reaching Up

....

_____

_____

_____

_____

_____

_____

_____

_____

_____

_____

_____

_____

_____

_____

_____

_____

_____

_____

_____

_____

_____

_____

DAY 17

In Need of a Deliverer

Then Peter said, "Silver or gold I do not have, but what I do have I give you. In the name of Jesus Christ of Nazareth, walk." Taking him by the right hand, he helped him up, and instantly the man's feet and ankles became strong. He jumped to his feet and began to walk. Then he went with them into the temple courts, walking and jumping, and praising God.

—ACTS 3:6-8

To get out of a pit, someone has to come to your rescue. You can opt for human help or you can opt for God. The fact that we could see our deliverer or have an audible conversation would be a decisive advantage. To see the look on a face or hear the tone in a voice—now that's real help. But that's not the kind of help we're talking about. God meant for people to offer one another a helping hand. The trouble comes when we insist upon someone equally human becoming our deliverer. Another person—rare though he may be—can pull us out from a pit but, for the life of him, he can't set us free.

Reflection Question

People can "help us," "lift us," and on occasion
"pull us" out of a pit, but what can't they do?

••••••••••••••••••••••••••••••••••••

_____

_____

_____

_____

_____

_____

_____

_____

_____

_____

_____

_____

_____

_____

_____

_____

_____

*Being confident of this, that he who began a good work in you
will carry it on to completion until the day of Christ Jesus.*
—PHILIPPIANS 1:6

Personal Application

What do Philippians 1:6 and 2 Corinthians 1:10 tell us about God's faithfulness? Which words in these verses mean the most to you personally, and why?

• •

_____

_____

_____

_____

_____

_____

_____

_____

_____

_____

_____

_____

_____

_____

_____

He has delivered us from such a deadly peril, and he will deliver us again. On him we have set our hope that he will continue to deliver us.
—2 CORINTHIANS 1:10

Reaching Up

....

_____

_____

_____

_____

_____

_____

_____

_____

_____

_____

_____

_____

_____

_____

_____

_____

_____

_____

_____

_____

_____

Out of the Pit and into Slavery

Judah said to his brothers, "What will we gain if we kill our brother and cover up his blood? Come, let's sell him to the Ishmaelites and not lay our hands on him; after all, he is our brother, our own flesh and blood." His brothers agreed. So when the Midianite merchants came by, his brothers pulled Joseph up out of the cistern and sold him for twenty shekels of silver to the Ishmaelites, who took him to Egypt.

—GENESIS 37:26–28

People can help us but they can't heal us. People can lift us but they can't carry us. On occasion people can pull us out of a pit, but they cannot keep us out. Nor can they set our feet upon a rock. If our idea of stability is standing on another human's shoulders, his clay feet will inevitably crumble and we'll take a tumble. The job's too big for him.

Joseph's brothers pulled him out of the cistern and sold him into slavery. In our relational parallel, if another person pulls us out of the pit, solely assuming the role of deliverer, he or she will inadvertently sell us into slavery of one kind or another almost every time.

Reflection Question

If a man—or a woman—assumes the sole role of our deliverer, what will he or she inadvertently do?

••••••••••••••••••••••••••••••••••••

_____

_____

_____

_____

_____

_____

_____

_____

_____

_____

_____

_____

_____

_____

_____

_____

_____

Yes, my soul, find rest in God;
my hope comes from him.
Truly he is my rock and my salvation;
he is my fortress, I will not be shaken.
—PSALM 62:5-6

Personal Application

What practical steps can you take to address the limitations of your friends, family members, professional counselor, minister, and support group?

•••••••••••••••••••••••••••••••••••

_____

_____

_____

_____

_____

_____

_____

_____

_____

_____

_____

_____

_____

_____

My salvation and my honor depend on God;
he is my mighty rock, my refuge.
Trust in him at all times, you people;
pour out your hearts to him,
for God is our refuge.
—PSALM 62:7-8

Reaching Up

....

_____

_____

_____

_____

_____

_____

_____

_____

_____

_____

_____

_____

_____

_____

_____

_____

_____

_____

_____

_____

_____

_____

Wounds from a Friend

Can the blind guide the blind? shall they not both fall into a pit?
—LUKE 6:39 ASV

We need a deliverer who is in for the long haul. Only God can hang with us through the length and depth of our need. Our human pit-pullers will run out of answers and energy and accidentally sell us into the slavery of nearly debilitating disappointment. When it happens, we reason that we might as well have stayed in the pit.

Sometimes a person abandons us not in spite of what we're going through, but directly because of it. If they wronged us only by running out of fuel and dropping out of the struggle, we might need to realize they've done all they felt they could humanly do and let them go without bitterness or anger.

Reflection Question

Why do some people abandon their hurting friends?

• •

_____

_____

_____

_____

_____

_____

_____

_____

_____

_____

_____

_____

_____

_____

_____

_____

_____

_____

_____

Sovereign LORD, my strong deliverer,
you shield my head in the day of battle.
—PSALM 140:7

Personal Application

Are you angry with someone in your life who you have
felt or feel has let you down? What role can forgiveness
play in helping you deal with hurt feelings?

● ●

_____

_____

_____

_____

_____

_____

_____

_____

_____

_____

_____

_____

As a father has compassion on his children,
so the LORD has compassion on those who fear him;
for he knows how we are formed,
he remembers that we are dust.

—PSALM 103:13–14

Reaching Up

....

_____

_____

_____

_____

_____

_____

_____

_____

_____

_____

_____

_____

_____

_____

_____

_____

_____

_____

_____

_____

_____

_____

Impacting a Life in the Pit

I urge you, brothers and sisters, by our Lord Jesus Christ and by the love
of the Spirit, to join me in my struggle by praying to God for me.
—ROMANS 15:30

We can have tremendous impact over a life in the pit. First of all, we can impact pit-dwellers by example. We can show them that living outside the pit is possible by living that way ourselves. Second, we can impact them by prayer. Third, we can impact pit-dwellers by encouragement. Satan has tremendous investment in convincing a person that sustainable victory is impossible. That's a lie. Say so. Fourth, we can doggedly direct them to Jesus. Like the men carrying the paralytic on the mat, do everything you can to "lay [the person] before Jesus" (Luke 5:18). Fifth, to the degree that God has developed biblical wisdom in us, we can impact pit-dwellers through our advice and counsel.

Reflection Question

If we can't pull someone out of a pit, what are five things we can do to "affect profound change in someone's life"?

●●●●●●●●●●●●●●●●●●●●●●●●●●●●●●●●●●●●●●

_____

_____

_____

_____

_____

_____

_____

_____

_____

_____

_____

_____

_____

_____

_____

And let us consider how we may spur one another on toward love and good deeds, not give up meeting together, as some are in the habit of doing, but encouraging one another—and all the more as you see the Day approaching.

—HEBREWS 10:24–25

Personal Application

Is there someone in your life you've been attempting
to rescue? If so, how do you think you should
relate to his or her problem from now on?

• •

_____

_____

_____

_____

_____

_____

_____

_____

_____

_____

_____

_____

_____

_____

_____

_____

But encourage one another daily, as long as it is called "Today,"
so that none of you may be hardened by sin's deceitfulness.
—HEBREWS 3:13

Reaching Up

....

_____

_____

_____

_____

_____

_____

_____

_____

_____

_____

_____

_____

_____

_____

_____

_____

_____

_____

_____

_____

DAY 21

You Can Opt for God

Now to him who is able to do immeasurably more than all
we ask or imagine, according to his power that is at work
within us, to him be glory in the church and in Christ Jesus
throughout all generations, for ever and ever! Amen.
—EPHESIANS 3:20-22

Pitching every other plan, you can opt for God. Oh, the wonder of the One who comes as Three! You can opt for the Father who reigns as King over every intricate detail in the universe and can micromanage a complicated life like yours and mine. You can opt for the Son who paid your debt in full, not just to deliver you from earth to heaven when you die, but also from pit to pavement while you live. You can opt for the Holy Spirit who infuses any willing vessel with throne-spilled power from the inside out. The One who enables people bereft of holiness to be holy by His very presence within them.

Reflection Question

"You can opt for God." What provisions do the
Father, the Son, and the Holy Spirit provide that
qualify them to pull someone out of a pit?

••••••••••••••••••••••••••••••••••

_____

_____

_____

_____

_____

_____

_____

_____

_____

_____

_____

_____

_____

_____

_____

_____

*And if the Spirit of him who raised Jesus from the dead is living
in you, he who raised Christ from the dead will also give life to
your mortal bodies because of his Spirit, who lives in you.*

—ROMANS 8:11

Personal Application

In order to get out of your pit, "God wants everything
you've got. Uncontested priority. Every egg in one basket.
All your weight on one limb." What would have to happen
in your life for you to take this challenge seriously?

• •

_____

_____

_____

_____

_____

_____

_____

_____

_____

_____

_____

_____

_____

_____

*The Spirit you received does not make you slaves, so that you live
in fear again; rather, the Spirit you received brought about your
adoption to sonship. And by him we cry, "Abba, Father."*

—ROMANS 8:15

Reaching Up

....

_____

_____

_____

_____

_____

_____

_____

_____

_____

_____

_____

_____

_____

_____

_____

_____

_____

_____

_____

_____

_____

_____

Cry Out

I waited patiently for the LORD;
he turned to me and heard my cry.

—PSALM 40:1

Deliverance begins with a cry erupting from a person's soul as if his or her life is dependent on it. This cry makes its first good use of the pit, aiming the petition straight up those narrow walls to the throne of God as if shot like fireworks from the cylinder of a Roman candle. The crier is aiming at the One who made all things, rules all things, and can change all things.

I believe God waits for the cry in order to remove all doubt about who came to our rescue. He won't let us claim circumstantial happenstance or saccharine philosophies like "Things have a way of working out." God works them out. Blessed is the one who knows it.

Reflection Question

Describe the kind of crying out a pit-dweller has to do. Why does God usually wait for us to cry out before rescuing us?

• •

_____

_____

_____

_____

_____

_____

_____

_____

_____

_____

_____

_____

_____

*The LORD said, "I have indeed seen the misery of my people in Egypt.
I have heard them crying out because of their slave drivers, and I am
concerned about their suffering. So I have come down to rescue them from
the hand of the Egyptians and to bring them up out of that land into a
good and spacious land, a land flowing with milk and honey—the home
of the Canaanites, Hittites, Amorites, Perizzites, Hivites and Jebusites.*
—EXODUS 3:7-8

Personal Application

If you are ready to begin your ascent from the pit,
what words would you use to cry out to God?

•••••••••••••••••••••••••••••••••••

_____

_____

_____

_____

_____

_____

_____

_____

_____

_____

_____

_____

_____

_____

_____

_____

_____

For he will deliver the needy who cry out,
the afflicted who have no one to help.
—PSALM 72:12

Reaching Up

....

_____

_____

_____

_____

_____

_____

_____

_____

_____

_____

_____

_____

_____

_____

_____

_____

_____

_____

_____

_____

_____

_____

Confess

If we claim to be without sin, we deceive ourselves and the truth is not in us. If we confess our sins, he is faithful and just and will forgive us our sins and purify us from all unrighteousness.
—1 JOHN 1:8-9

After you cry out, *confess*. Confession takes place every time you tell God how much you need Him. Tell Him what's on your mind. What kind of mess you're in. Who's in it with you. What's holding you back. What's on your heart. Who's on your case. Who's made you mad. Who's on your nerves. Who's broken your heart. Even if you think it's Him. As long as you can feel it, spill it. Don't overlook the unparalleled benefit of confessing sin. Let His light shine on it so the two of you can sort it out and He can heal you. Don't leave out sins of pride. Nothing contributes more to the length of our stay in the pit.

Reflection Question

"After you cry out, *confess.*" What does our confession include?

• •

_____

_____

_____

_____

_____

_____

_____

_____

_____

_____

_____

_____

_____

_____

_____

_____

_____

_____

The LORD is near to all who call on him,
to all who call on him in truth.

—PSALM 145:18

Personal Application

What do you need to confess to God? What
attitude, motive, and/or action can you think of
that contributed to your being in a pit?

••••••••••••••••••••••••••••••••••

_____

_____

_____

_____

_____

_____

_____

_____

_____

_____

_____

_____

_____

_____

Who is a God like you,
who pardons sin and forgives the transgression
of the remnant of his inheritance?
You do not stay angry forever
but delight to show mercy.
—MICAH 7:18

Reaching Up

·······································

_____

_____

_____

_____

_____

_____

_____

_____

_____

_____

_____

_____

_____

_____

_____

_____

_____

_____

_____

_____

_____

Consent

*This is the confidence we have in approaching God: that if we ask
anything according to his will, he hears us. And if we know that he hears
us—whatever we ask—we know that we have what we asked of him.*
—1 JOHN 5:14–15

C ry out. Confess. Consent. The definition of the noun form
of *consent* is: "Compliance in or approval of what is done or
proposed by another . . . agreement as to action or opinion . . .
voluntary agreement."[1] *Consent* is the most beautiful part of the
process of getting out of a pit. There is no ambiguity about this
step; it is definitely God's will. Determining God's will in so many
other areas is less than certain. This one's black-and-white. God's
will is for you to get out of that pit. If you will consent to the
process, waiting upon God as He begins shifting, shoving, and
rearranging things for your release, you can go ahead and start
getting excited because it will happen.

Reflection Question

After we confess, consent. What does consent
mean in this case? To what must we consent?

•••••••••••••••••••••••••••••••••••••

_____

_____

_____

_____

_____

_____

_____

_____

_____

_____

_____

_____

_____

_____

_____

_____

_____

_____

_____

So faith comes from hearing, and hearing by the word of Christ.
—ROMANS 10:17 NASB

Personal Application

What will it mean for you to "actively consent" to getting out of your pit?

••••••••••••••••••••••••••••••••••••

_____

_____

_____

_____

_____

_____

_____

_____

_____

Praise the LORD, my soul;
all my inmost being, praise his holy name.
Praise the LORD, my soul,
and forget not all his benefits—
who forgives all your sins
and heals all your diseases,
who redeems your life from the pit
and crowns you with love and compassion,
who satisfies your desires with good things
so that your youth is renewed like the eagle's.

—PSALM 103:1–5

Reaching Up

....

_____
_____
_____
_____
_____
_____
_____
_____
_____
_____
_____
_____
_____
_____
_____
_____
_____
_____
_____
_____
_____
_____
_____

DAY 25

Driven by Relationship

*About midnight Paul and Silas were praying and singing hymns to God,
and the other prisoners were listening to them. Suddenly there was such
a violent earthquake that the foundations of the prison were shaken. At
once all the prison doors flew open, and everyone's chains came loose.*

—ACTS 16:25-26

God can deliver us instantly, but I think He enjoys the togetherness of the wait. Not too long ago one of our best friends nearly died. His closest friends hovered at the ICU door for days. We had not been together like that in years. Hadn't had time. Suddenly we made time.

Relationship. That's one of the best things that can come out of a waiting room. Even the faith in God that an intense wait demands is about relationship. God calls us to walk in faith because faith requires a partner to place it in. It takes two to tango out of a pit. His part is to lift you out. Your part is to hold on for dear life.

Reflection Question

God is driven by relationship. In terms of getting out
of a pit, what is His part, and what is our part?

•••••••••••••••••••••••••••••••••••••

_____

_____

_____

_____

_____

_____

_____

_____

_____

_____

_____

_____

_____

_____

_____

_____

_____

_____

I wait for the LORD, my whole being waits,
and in his word I put my hope.
—PSALM 130:5

Personal Application

God can deliver a person instantaneously, but this is a rare occurrence. Has this ever happened to you or to someone you know? What was your response? Were you awed by God's power? Skeptical? Reassured?

· ·

_____

_____

_____

_____

_____

_____

_____

_____

_____

_____

_____

_____

_____

_____

Israel, put your hope in the LORD,
for with the LORD is unfailing love
and with him is full redemption.
—PSALM 130:7

Reaching Up

....

_____

_____

_____

_____

_____

_____

_____

_____

_____

_____

_____

_____

_____

_____

_____

_____

_____

_____

_____

_____

_____

_____

_____

While You Wait

I wait for the Lord
more than watchmen wait for the morning,
more than watchmen wait for the morning.
—PSALM 130:6

Deliverance didn't happen instantaneously for the psalmist who wrote, "I waited patiently for the LORD; / he turned to me and heard my cry. / He lifted me out of the slimy pit, / out of the mud and mire" (Psalm 40:1–2).

We may have to wait for deliverance, but we never have to wait on God Himself. Never have to wait to enjoy His presence or be reassured of His love. We can take God at His Word and have any one of those relational delights instantly. The only wait is on seeing His work manifest in the physical realm, seeing our petition come to fruition.

Reflection Question

Most of the time we have to wait patiently for
deliverance from our pits, but during the wait, what
are some things for which we never have to wait?

••••••••••••••••••••••••••••••••••

_____

_____

_____

_____

_____

_____

_____

_____

_____

_____

_____

_____

_____

_____

_____

_____

_____

But the fruit of the Spirit is love, joy, peace, forbearance, kindness, goodness,
faithfulness, gentleness and self-control. Against such things there is no law.

—GALATIANS 5:22-23

Personal Application

As you have waited for God to deliver you, what
has been your frame of mind? Compare yours with
the psalmists' in Psalm 40:1–2 and 130:5–6.

• •

_____

_____

_____

_____

_____

_____

_____

_____

_____

_____

_____

Hear my cry for help,

my King and my God,

for to you I pray.

In the morning, LORD, you hear my voice;

in the morning I lay my requests before you

and wait expectantly.

—PSALM 5:2-3

Reaching Up

....

Signs of Deliverance

Do not gloat over me, my enemy!
Though I have fallen, I will rise.
Though I sit in darkness,
the LORD will be my light.

—MICAH 7:8

Despite appearances, huge things happen as you wait upon the Lord to deliver you from that pit. They begin when you cry out. You can tell the process is well underway the moment you begin reversing the three characteristics of a pit: you feel stuck, you can't stand up, you've lost your vision. When you are convinced that you're no longer hopelessly stuck (you proved that when you cried out), when you resume a standing position against the Enemy (you did that when you began confessing truth and consenting to God), and you're regaining glimpses of vision (you realize God doesn't hate you nor is He, worse, oblivious to you), you're no longer in the dark of the deep.

Reflection Question

What are some signs that our deliverance
process is well underway?

....

_____

_____

_____

_____

_____

_____

_____

_____

_____

_____

_____

_____

_____

_____

_____

Since you are my rock and my fortress,
for the sake of your name lead and guide me.
Keep me free from the trap that is set for me,
for you are my refuge.

—PSALM 31:3-4

Personal Application

"But smooth living invariably, eventually, makes
for sloppy spirituality." Can you think of a time
in your life when this was especially true?

• •

_____

_____

_____

_____

_____

_____

_____

_____

_____

_____

_____

_____

*Therefore put on the full armor of God, so that when the
day of evil comes, you may be able to stand your ground,
and after you have done everything, to stand.*
—EPHESIANS 6:13

Reaching Up

....

_____

_____

_____

_____

_____

_____

_____

_____

_____

_____

_____

_____

_____

_____

_____

_____

_____

_____

_____

_____

_____

_____

DAY 28

Absolute Expectation

For when you did awesome things that we did not expect,
you came down, and the mountains trembled before you.
—ISAIAH 64:3

The psalmist who "waited patiently for the LORD" (Psalm 40:1) didn't sit around in the mire, sinking deeper every minute, telling God to take His time. The phrase "waited patiently" is translated from the Hebrew word *qwh*.[1] *Qwh* is translated "expect" in Isaiah 64:3: "For when you did awesome things that we did not expect, / you came down, and the mountains trembled before you." The psalmist didn't sit in the pit and twiddle his muddy thumbs until God delivered him. He postured himself in absolute expectation. He had a goal, and his shoulders would not slump till he saw it fulfilled. His Deliverer was coming and, on His way, fighting battles and blazing paths somewhere beyond the psalmist's gaze.

Reflection Question

Read Psalm 40:1–2. What is the true meaning of the Hebrew term *qwh* that we translate as "wait"? Describe a person who is waiting for the Lord as the Hebrew psalmist meant it.

....

_____

_____

_____

_____

_____

_____

_____

_____

_____

_____

_____

I waited patiently for the LORD;
he turned to me and heard my cry.
He lifted me out of the slimy pit,
out of the mud and mire;
he set my feet on a rock
and gave me a firm place to stand.
—PSALM 40:1-2

Personal Application

Psalm 130:5 says, "In his word I put my hope." In the past, where have you placed your hope? What is one thing you can do while you wait and hope for deliverance?

••••••••••••••••••••••••••••••••••

_____

_____

_____

_____

_____

_____

_____

_____

_____

_____

_____

_____

_____

_____

For since the beginning of the world
Men have not heard nor perceived by the ear,
Nor has the eye seen any God besides You,
Who acts for the one who waits for Him.
—ISAIAH 64:4 NKJV

Reaching Up

....

_____

_____

_____

_____

_____

_____

_____

_____

_____

_____

_____

_____

_____

_____

_____

_____

_____

_____

_____

_____

_____

_____

DAY 29

A Firm Place to Stay

Every good and perfect gift is from above, coming down from the Father
of the heavenly lights, who does not change like shifting shadows.
—JAMES 1:17

God is not just a firm place to stand on. He's a firm place to stay on. If we want out of the pit for good, we've got to make up our minds. The ground beneath our feet will be only as firm as our resolve. As long as we're wishy-washy, what's under us will be wishy-washy too.

God *gives* us a firm place to stand, but we have to decide we want to take it. John 3:16 tells us that God gave us His Son, but He doesn't force anyone to take Him either. God is ever the Giver (see James 1:17) but, by His sovereign design, each individual gets to exercise the prerogative whether or not to be a recipient.

Reflection Question

If we truly want to get out of a pit for good, what is
the one absolutely crucial thing we must do?

....

_____

_____

_____

_____

_____

_____

_____

_____

_____

_____

_____

_____

_____

_____

_____

_____

_____

_____

_____

For God so loved the world that he gave his one and only Son, that
whoever believes in him shall not perish but have eternal life.

—JOHN 3:16

Personal Application

What are some of the inevitable temptations you can
expect to face in the next few days, weeks, or months
as you attempt to stand firmly on your Rock?

••••••••••••••••••••••••••••••••••••

_____

_____

_____

_____

_____

_____

_____

_____

_____

_____

_____

_____

_____

*No temptation has overtaken you except what is common to
mankind. And God is faithful; he will not let you be tempted
beyond what you can bear. But when you are tempted, he
will also provide a way out so that you can endure it.*
—1 CORINTHIANS 10:13

Reaching Up

....

_____

_____

_____

_____

_____

_____

_____

_____

_____

_____

_____

_____

_____

_____

_____

_____

_____

_____

_____

_____

_____

_____

_____

Make Up Your Mind

Then they would put their trust in God
and would not forget his deeds
but would keep his commands.
They would not be like their ancestors—
a stubborn and rebellious generation,
whose hearts were not loyal to God,
whose spirits were not faithful to him.
—PSALM 78:7-8

We've got to settle some things in advance of the inevitable temptation to revert or destructively scratch a temporary itch. We can't wait until the heat of the moment to decide. A loyal spouse doesn't wait until someone flirts with her to choose faithfulness. She made the decision before the circumstance arose.

God offers you a firm place to stand on, but your feet are not firmly in place until you've made up your mind that's where you want to be. He will not force you to stand or stay. Until you finally make up your mind that you're cleaving to God and calling upon His power from now until hades freezes over, your feet are set upon a banana peel.

Reflection Question

In order to stay out of a pit, why is it important to have
certain questions answered before life asks them; some
things settled in advance of the inevitable temptation
to revert or destructively scratch a temporary itch?

....

_____

_____

_____

_____

_____

_____

_____

_____

_____

_____

_____

_____

_____

_____

_____

"Watch and pray so that you will not fall into temptation.
The spirit is willing, but the flesh is weak."

—MATTHEW 26:41

Personal Application

"We must settle some things in advance." When the next temptations arise, what might you say or do differently that indicates you have "made up your mind"?

· ·

_____

_____

_____

_____

_____

_____

_____

_____

_____

_____

_____

_____

_____

_____

Teach me your way, Lord,
that I may rely on your faithfulness;
give me an undivided heart,
that I may fear your name.
—PSALM 86:11

Reaching Up

....

_____

_____

_____

_____

_____

_____

_____

_____

_____

_____

_____

_____

_____

_____

_____

_____

_____

_____

_____

_____

_____

_____

Getting Out When They Stay In

To him who is able to keep you from stumbling and to present you
before his glorious presence without fault and with great joy—to the
only God our Savior be glory, majesty, power and authority, through
Jesus Christ our Lord, before all ages, now and forevermore! Amen.
—JUDE 1:24-25

There's nothing quite like trying to stay out of a pit while your loved ones are still in it. A whole family or set of friends can take up residency in a deluxe-sized pit. If you're the first one who escapes, you'd think your fellow pit-dwellers would be happy that at least you got out. But although your deliverance should give them hopes of their own, someone usually feels betrayed that you felt a change was necessary. They think it means you're saying something is wrong with the rest of them. Sometimes when a person decides to have a mind made up toward God and feet firmly set upon a rock, loyalty to Him is misinterpreted as disloyalty to the family.

Reflection Question

Why is staying out of a pit, while others close to us
are still in one, often the biggest challenge of all?

....

_____

_____

_____

_____

_____

_____

_____

_____

_____

_____

_____

_____

_____

_____

_____

Who shall separate us from the love of Christ? Shall trouble or
hardship or persecution or famine or nakedness or danger or sword?
As it is written: "For your sake we face death all day long; we
are considered as sheep to be slaughtered." No, in all these things
we are more than conquerors through him who loved us.

—ROMANS 8:35–37

Personal Application

Which relationships in your life will have to change as a result
of your resolve to stay out of the pit? How will your family
change? How will your relationships with friends change?

•••••••••••••••••••••••••••••••••

_____

_____

_____

_____

_____

_____

_____

_____

_____

_____

_____

_____

_____

*For I am convinced that neither death nor life, neither angels nor
demons, neither the present nor the future, nor any powers, neither
height nor depth, nor anything else in all creation, will be able to
separate us from the love of God that is in Christ Jesus our Lord.*
—ROMANS 8:38-39

Reaching Up

....

The Nature of Relationships

Remember that you were slaves in Egypt and that the LORD your God
brought you out of there with a mighty hand and an outstretched arm.
—DEUTERONOMY 5:15

The nature of some of our closest relationships changes when God performs a dramatic deliverance in our lives. The healthier we get, the more we realize how unhealthy we were. We find out who has been a false Christ to us and how we may have been a false Christ to others. We find out where we've been motivated by guilt more than God.

Some relationships won't survive your deliverance. And most of them don't need to. You discover that the pit was all you had in common. Under different circumstances you wouldn't even have been drawn together. If it's not a relationship God blesses, and not one His Word binds you to (like your marriage), it needs candid examination.

Reflection Question

When God performs a dramatic deliverance in our lives, what are some of the changes we can expect in our relationships?

....

_____

_____

_____

_____

_____

_____

_____

_____

_____

_____

_____

_____

_____

_____

_____

_____

Therefore, since we have been justified through faith, we have peace with God through our Lord Jesus Christ, through whom we have gained access by faith into this grace in which we now stand. And we boast in the hope of the glory of God.

—ROMANS 5:1-2

Personal Application

Is there a relationship in your life that is fueled by addiction or is in danger of becoming so? Is this a relationship that you must end? Why or why not?

••••••••••••••••••••••••••••••••

_____

_____

_____

_____

_____

_____

_____

_____

_____

_____

_____

_____

_____

_____

_____

*And this is my prayer: that your love may abound more and more in
knowledge and depth of insight, so that you may be able to discern
what is best and may be pure and blameless for the day of Christ.*
—PHILIPPIANS 1:9–10

Reaching Up

....

_____

_____

_____

_____

_____

_____

_____

_____

_____

_____

_____

_____

_____

_____

_____

_____

_____

_____

_____

_____

DAY 33

A New Song in Your Mouth

He put a new song in my mouth,
a hymn of praise to our God.
Many will see and fear the LORD
and put their trust in him.

—PSALM 40:3

You will have a new song in your mouth—that's the second way you'll know you've waved goodbye to the pit. Right after the psalmist tells us that God sets us on the rock and gives us a firm place to stand, he tells us God gives us a new song: "He put a new song in my mouth, a hymn of praise to our God" (Psalm 40:3).

Every one of us was born for a song. Even the one who can't carry a tune in a bucket. Even the one who wouldn't mind church so much if it weren't for the singing. The one who just doesn't get it—and doesn't think she wants to.

Reflection Question

Right after God sets us on the rock and gives us
a firm place to stand, what, according to Psalm
40:3, is the very next thing He does?

....

_____

_____

_____

_____

_____

_____

_____

_____

"I have swept away your offenses like a cloud,
your sins like the morning mist.
Return to me,
for I have redeemed you."
Sing for joy, you heavens, for the LORD has done this;
shout aloud, you earth beneath.
Burst into song, you mountains,
you forests and all your trees,
for the LORD has redeemed Jacob,
he displays his glory in Israel.
—ISAIAH 44:22–23

Personal Application

Have you begun to hear a God-song in your heart? Can you put words to your song? If it is an actual song that you can sing, sing it!

••••••••••••••••••••••••••••••••

_____

_____

_____

_____

_____

_____

_____

_____

_____

_____

_____

_____

_____

_____

_____

Speaking to one another with psalms, hymns, and songs from the Spirit.
Sing and make music from your heart to the Lord, always giving thanks
to God the Father for everything, in the name of our Lord Jesus Christ.
—EPHESIANS 5:19–20

Reaching Up

· ·

_____

_____

_____

_____

_____

_____

_____

_____

_____

_____

_____

_____

_____

_____

_____

_____

_____

_____

_____

_____

_____

_____

_____

DAY 34

A God-Song

Sing to the LORD a new song,
for he has done marvelous things;
his right hand and his holy arm
have worked salvation for him.
—PSALM 98:1

You were born for a God-song. Your heart beats to its rhythm and your vocal cords were fashioned to give it volume. A God-song in the simplest man's soul is greater than any symphony. It's more than emotional intoxication or getting lost in the moment. It's the unleashed anthem of a freed soul. A song expresses something no amount of spoken words can articulate. No amount of nonverbal affection can demonstrate. Music is its own thing, especially when instruments and voices respond to the tap of the divine Conductor. Nothing can take a song's place. If the outlet gets clogged, the soul gets heavier and heavier. And nothing on earth clogs the windpipe like the polluted air of a pit.

Reflection Question

"Your heart beats to the rhythm of a God-song, and your vocal cords were fashioned to give it volume." What is a God-song?

••••••••••••••••••••••••••••••••••

_____

_____

_____

_____

_____

_____

_____

_____

_____

_____

_____

_____

My heart, O God, is steadfast,
my heart is steadfast;
I will sing and make music.
Awake, my soul!
Awake, harp and lyre!
I will awaken the dawn.

—PSALM 57:7-8

Personal Application

When you're in a pit, you may be singing a song, but it's usually not a God-song. What are some of the Enemy's songs that you've been singing? If you can't think of an actual song, make up a song title that fits your situation. (Think country, and have fun with this!)

• •

_____

_____

_____

_____

_____

_____

_____

_____

_____

_____

_____

_____

_____

_____

I will praise you, LORD, with all my heart;
before the "gods" I will sing your praise.
—PSALM 138:1

Reaching Up

....

_____
_____
_____
_____
_____
_____
_____
_____
_____
_____
_____
_____
_____
_____
_____
_____
_____
_____
_____
_____
_____
_____
_____

Singing Through the Pain

About midnight Paul and Silas were praying and singing hymns
to God, and the other prisoners were listening to them.
—ACTS 16:25

A song of praise freely sung and spontaneously offered is one of the most blatant trademarks of joy in tribulation. However, having a new song in our mouths doesn't mean we're completely out of the pain that caused our pit or the pain that our pit caused. It doesn't even mean, if ours was a pit of sin, that the consequences are necessarily behind us. It just means we're no longer stuck. No longer defeated. No longer caked in mud. Our vision is returning. Hints of creativity are reemerging. It's a new day, God doesn't hate us after all, and we can't help but praise. The wind is blowing in our faces once again and once more hope springs eternal.

Reflection Question

If having a new song in our mouths does not mean we
are completely free from pain, what does it mean?

....

_____

_____

_____

_____

_____

_____

_____

_____

_____

_____

_____

_____

_____

_____

_____

_____

Because of the LORD's great love we are not consumed,
for his compassions never fail.
They are new every morning;
great is your faithfulness.
—LAMENTATIONS 3:22-23

Personal Application

Describe a time when you spontaneously began singing a song of praise—maybe in your car, at home, in an elevator, etc. Also describe a time when you sang, not because you felt like it, but as an act of faith. What was the result of your singing?

....

_____

_____

_____

_____

_____

_____

_____

_____

I will give you thanks, for you answered me;
you have become my salvation.
The stone the builders rejected
has become the cornerstone;
the LORD has done this,
and it is marvelous in our eyes.
The LORD has done it this very day;
let us rejoice today and be glad.
—PSALM 118:21-24

Reaching Up

∙∙∙∙∙∙∙∙∙∙∙∙∙∙∙∙∙∙∙∙∙∙∙∙∙∙∙∙∙∙∙∙∙∙∙∙∙

_____

_____

_____

_____

_____

_____

_____

_____

_____

_____

_____

_____

_____

_____

_____

_____

_____

_____

_____

_____

_____

_____

_____

_____

_____

DAY 36

Songs of Deliverance

Those who sow with tears
will reap with songs of joy.
Those who go out weeping,
carrying seed to sow,
will return with songs of joy,
carrying sheaves with them.
—PSALM 126:5-6

Carrie McDonnall lost her husband and three friends on the streets of Iraq when the vehicle carrying the Christian relief workers was sprayed with gunfire. She was the lone survivor. During her recovery, God opened her ears to hear the music of heaven. She described the music like a choir of countless voices with one set of harmony in one ear and another totally distinguishable set in the other.

The glorious songs of heaven are unceasingly sung. While we can't hear them, we can know they're being sung. And never more vividly than when a person is being delivered. Psalm 32:7 says, "You are my hiding place; / you will protect me from trouble / and surround me with songs of deliverance."

Reflection Question

How can we know the songs of heaven are unceasingly
sung as accompaniment on our journey out of the pit?

• •

_____

_____

_____

_____

_____

_____

_____

_____

_____

_____

_____

_____

_____

_____

_____

_____

You are my hiding place;
you will protect me from trouble
and surround me with songs of deliverance.
—PSALM 32:7

Personal Application

Now, pick one or two songs and/or soundtracks that you think God might use to accompany your victorious deliverance from a pit. Try to play them every day. While you're listening, picture in your mind the dramatic moment of your victory over the deadly pit from which you're now emerging—or soon will be.

∙∙∙∙∙∙∙∙∙∙∙∙∙∙∙∙∙∙∙∙∙∙∙∙∙∙∙∙∙∙∙∙∙∙∙∙

_____

_____

_____

_____

_____

_____

_____

_____

_____

Shout for joy to the LORD, all the earth.
Worship the LORD with gladness;
come before him with joyful songs.
Know that the LORD is God.
It is he who made us, and we are his;
we are his people, the sheep of his pasture.
—PSALM 100:1-3

Reaching Up

....

_____

_____

_____

_____

_____

_____

_____

_____

_____

_____

_____

_____

_____

_____

_____

_____

_____

_____

_____

_____

_____

_____

_____

_____

DAY 37

What's This World Coming To?

*Then I saw "a new heaven and a new earth," for the first heaven and
the first earth had passed away, and there was no longer any sea. I
saw the Holy City, the new Jerusalem, coming down out of heaven
from God, prepared as a bride beautifully dressed for her husband.*

—REVELATION 21:1–2

If we live long enough and stay plugged in, we end up asking the same question our parents and grandparents asked: what's this world coming to? According to Revelation 21, earth as we know it will come to an end and God will usher into existence a new heaven and new earth with properties beyond our wildest imagination.

Most folks agree that heaven is a better option than hell but, comparatively speaking, only a handful of Christians really anticipate their futures there. We're scared to death that it's going to be like our church services, only instead of getting out at noon, it will last an eternity. We can't picture how anything holy can possibly be lively. Let alone fun.

Reflection Question

According to Revelation 21:1–6, what will eventually happen to the world (the first earth as we know it)? What will replace it?

....

_____
_____
_____
_____
_____
_____
_____
_____
_____
_____
_____
_____
_____
_____
_____

And I heard a loud voice from the throne saying, "Look! God's dwelling place is now among the people, and he will dwell with them. They will be his people, and God himself will be with them and be their God. He will wipe every tear from their eyes. There will be no more death or mourning or crying or pain, for the old order of things has passed away."

—REVELATION 21:3-4

Personal Application

What comes to mind when you try to answer the
question, "What's this world coming to?"

• •

_____

_____

_____

_____

_____

_____

_____

_____

_____

_____

_____

_____

_____

_____

*He who was seated on the throne said, "I am making everything
new!" Then he said, "Write this down, for these words are
trustworthy and true." He said to me: "It is done. I am the Alpha
and the Omega, the Beginning and the End. To the thirsty I will
give water without cost from the spring of the water of life."*

—REVELATION 21:5-6

Reaching Up

....

Springs of Living Water

Meanwhile we groan, longing to be clothed instead with our heavenly dwelling, because when we are clothed, we will not be found naked. For while we are in this tent, we groan and are burdened, because we do not wish to be unclothed but to be clothed instead with our heavenly dwelling, so that what is mortal may be swallowed up by life. Now the one who has fashioned us for this very purpose is God, who has given us the Spirit as a deposit, guaranteeing what is to come.
—2 CORINTHIANS 5:2–5

Psalm 23:1–3 says, "The LORD is my shepherd; / I shall not want. / He makes me to lie down in green pastures; / He leads me beside the still waters. / He restores my soul" (NKJV). Revelation 7:17 says, "For the Lamb at the center of the throne will be their shepherd; 'he will lead them to springs of living water.'" Get a load of that: Still waters on earth. Springs of living water in heaven. Compared to the whitewater existence we'll have in heaven, here we're like toads perched on the lily pad of a stagnant pond. Heaven is where all the action is. Every sunrise, sunset, season change, mountain range, forest, and foaming sea on earth is a mere shadow of heaven.

Reflection Question

Comparing Psalm 23:1–3 with Revelation 7:17, how
will life in heaven be different from life on earth?

••••••••••••••••••••••••••••••••

_____

_____

_____

_____

_____

_____

_____

_____

_____

_____

_____

_____

_____

_____

_____

*No longer will there be any curse. The throne of God and of the
Lamb will be in the city, and his servants will serve him. They
will see his face, and his name will be on their foreheads.*

—REVELATION 22:3-4

Personal Application

When you read Revelation 21:1–4, what are your feelings?
Describe how your life might one day be—without pain or tears.

••••••••••••••••••••••••••••••••••••

_____

_____

_____

_____

_____

_____

_____

_____

_____

_____

_____

_____

_____

_____

_____

_____

_____

*There will be no more night. They will not need the light
of a lamp or the light of the sun, for the Lord God will give
them light. And they will reign for ever and ever.*
—REVELATION 22:5

Reaching Up

....

_____

_____
_____
_____
_____
_____
_____
_____
_____
_____
_____
_____
_____
_____
_____
_____
_____
_____
_____
_____
_____
_____
_____
_____
_____
_____

A Bottomless Pit

Then I saw an angel coming down from heaven, having the key to
the bottomless pit and a great chain in his hand. He laid hold of
the dragon, that serpent of old, who is the Devil and Satan, and
bound him for a thousand years; and he cast him into the bottomless
pit, and shut him up, and set a seal on him, so that he should
deceive the nations no more till the thousand years were finished.
But after these things he must be released for a little while.
—REVELATION 20:1–3 NKJV

Before the Lord does away with Satan once and for all, He's going to give him a taste of the pit—the bottomless pit (see Revelation 20:3). It's the perfect plan, really. And sublimely scriptural. Long ago Psalm 7:15–16 promised that "whoever digs a hole and scoops it out / falls into the pit they have made. / The trouble they cause recoils on them; / their violence comes down on their own heads." In God's economy, those who dig a pit for others will fall into it themselves (see Psalm 57:6). Maybe the reason Satan's pit is so deep is because God is scooping it out until it reaches the total depth of all the ones the devil dug for us.

Reflection Question

In God's economy, what happens to
those who dig a pit for others?

• •

_____

_____

_____

_____

_____

_____

_____

_____

_____

_____

_____

_____

_____

_____

They spread a net for my feet—
I was bowed down in distress.
They dug a pit in my path—
but they have fallen into it themselves.
—PSALM 57:6

Personal Application

What specific decisions have you made that will help you get out of your pit? Write them down and put your list in a prominent place as inspiration for your victorious life—out of the pit!

••••••••••••••••••••••••••••••••••

_____

_____

_____

_____

_____

_____

_____

_____

_____

_____

_____

_____

_____

_____

_____

Whoever digs a hole and scoops it out
falls into the pit they have made.
The trouble they cause recoils on them;
their violence comes down on their own heads.

—PSALM 7:15-16

Reaching Up

....

_____

_____

_____

_____

_____

_____

_____

_____

_____

_____

_____

_____

_____

_____

_____

_____

_____

_____

_____

_____

_____

Basking in the Son

My beloved spake, and said unto me, Rise up,
my love, my fair one, and come away.
—SONG OF SOLOMON 2:10 KJV

By the time Satan looks at life from his bottomless pit, our feet will forever be firmly set upon a rock. The air will be clear. The view crystal. The fellowship sweet. And the sufferings of this present time won't even be worthy to compare to the glory revealed to us (see Romans 8:18). We'll ride raftless in rivers of living waters then bask in the Son.

Until then, life on this battered earth will not be easy, but we never have to make another bed in the bottom of a pit. We'll have bad days, mind you. But when we're feeling the familiar pull of a pit, Christ will stretch out His mighty arm and say, "Need a hand?"

Reflection Question

What does Romans 8:18 promise us in
terms of our present suffering?

....

_____

_____

_____

_____

_____

_____

_____

_____

_____

_____

_____

_____

_____

_____

_____

_____

_____

*I consider that our present sufferings are not worth
comparing with the glory that will be revealed in us.*

—ROMANS 8:18

Personal Application

Have you decided to take the hand of Christ and be released from your pit? If so, do it now by praying a prayer, giving your life to Him, and asking Him to be your Savior and Lord.

· ·

_____

_____

_____

_____

_____

_____

_____

_____

_____

_____

_____

_____

If you declare with your mouth, "Jesus is Lord," and believe in your heart that God raised him from the dead, you will be saved. For it is with your heart that you believe and are justified, and it is with your mouth that you profess your faith and are saved. As Scripture says, "Anyone who believes in him will never be put to shame."

—ROMANS 10:9–11

Reaching Up

....

_____

_____

_____

_____

_____

_____

_____

_____

_____

_____

_____

_____

_____

_____

_____

_____

_____

_____

_____

_____

Notes

Day 24: Consent
1. *Merriam-Webster Collegiate Dictionary*, 10th ed., s.v. "consent."

Day 28: Absolute Expectation
1. Spiros Zodhiates, ed., "Lexical Aids to the Old Testament,"
   The Hebrew-Greek Key Word Study Bible, #7744
   (Chattanooga, TN: AMG Publishers, 1998), 1,548.

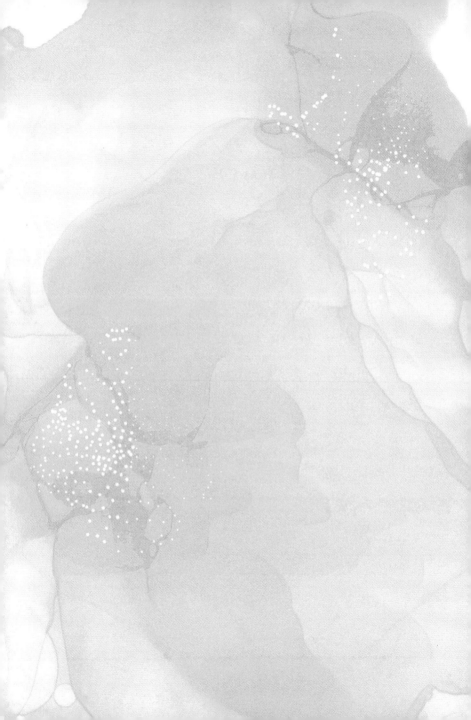

About the Author

Author and speaker Beth Moore is a dynamic teacher whose conferences take her across the globe. She has written numerous bestselling books and Bible studies. She is also the founder and visionary of Living Proof Ministries based in Houston, Texas. Born in Green Bay, Wisconsin, she is the fourth child of a retired Army major and a homemaker. Before the family moved to Houston in her teen years, Beth spent most of her childhood in Arkadelphia, Arkansas, where her father managed the local cinema. Beth currently enjoys life in the woods outside of Houston with her husband, Keith. She is an avid reader and loves Tex-Mex, catching a movie, and being a grandmother to her three delightful grandchildren.

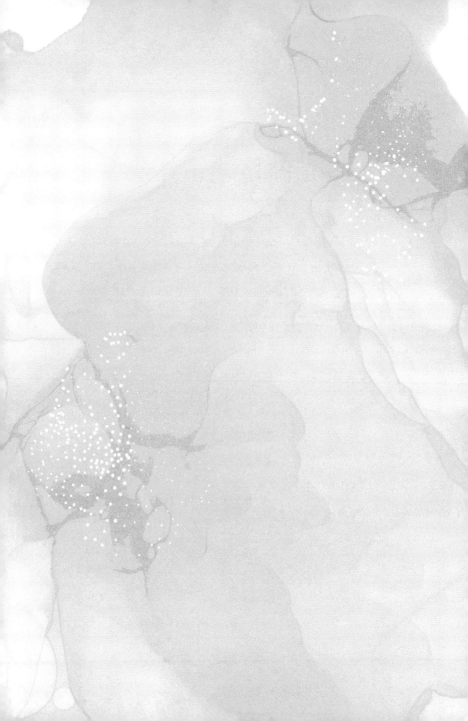